Norwegian Trivia Book

Interesting and Fun Facts About Norwegian Culture, History, Tourist Attractions, and Much More

Alex Anderson

Contents

Introduction 3

Chapter One - Norwegian Culture and Society 5

Chapter Two - Norwegian History......... 18

Chapter Three - Norwegian Geography . 33

Chapter Four - Popular Norwegian Tourist Attraction Trivia 49

Conclusion 69

References 71

Introduction

Norway, the Land of the Midnight Sun, is officially known as Kongeriket Norge, or Kingdom of Norway. It is a wondrous country seamlessly combining the modern, millennial culture, rich history, and a beautiful but harsh climate, not to mention boasting of a high standard of living. The Scandinavian gods were born in Norway, as were the Vikings.

Today, Norway is a gateway to the northernmost expanses of Europe. There is something in Norway for every kind of traveler: those who seek history, nature lovers, food connoisseurs, lovers of art and literature, and leisure seekers. The inimitable Norwegian fjords that dot the landscape and the wondrous beauty of the Northern Lights are not the only things Norway has to offer.

This trivia book is written to spread awareness about the one and only Norway, whose fame is not limited to being a "capitalist country with a conscience." This book gives the facts without the boredom usually associated with pedantic learning.

Go on, impress your family and friends at parties and social gatherings with some wonderful but less-known trivia about Norway. Whether you are preparing for a quiz night as a quiz master or a participant, this Norway trivia book will be useful to you. So, go on, turn the page, and dive straight in.

Chapter One - Norwegian Culture and Society

Norway was once called Norweg, which means "the Northern Way." With a population of nearly 5.5 million, Norway is located in Scandinavia. Norwegian society, in the ancient days, consisted of three tiers. The bottom-most tier belonged to those people who did the most difficult and abhorrent tasks, and these people were mostly slaves. The middle tier belonged to freemen, and their status in society depended on the land they owned. The first tier of society belonged to the nobility.

Today, all are equal in the democratic setup, and the first thing that comes to mind about Norwegian culture and society is Allemannsretten.

Allemannsretten is the Norwegian Way of Life

Allemannsretten means "everyone, man and woman, has the right to public access," and this is an important cultural belief in Norway. This word refers to the "freedom to roam anywhere in Norway." The literal translation is "every man's right." This law empowers everyone to roam free and unhindered on any uncultivated land in Norway. At this point, you must remember that every right comes with a corresponding duty, and therefore, the limitations of Allemannsretten include the following:

- It is your duty to respect nature, which means you cannot litter anywhere or disturb wildlife in any way. You are expected to leave nature as you found it.
- You can hike or set up camp in any uncultivated land as long as you don't disturb anyone and are at least 150 m away from private properties. And if your camp is more than 2 days old, you must seek permission from the local inhabitants of that land. Remote areas and mountains are exempt from the 2-day limit.
- Campfires are disallowed in forest areas during summers.
- Fishing in saltwater is allowed in small boats, provided it is for personal use only.

The thing is that Norway is one big campsite as long as you know how to respect the freedom and privacy of others.

Norway Is the World's Most Well-Read Country

Norwegians love their books and literature, which is reflected in the fact that they read more than any other nation in the world. Over 2,000 books are published every year in this country. The government also encourages readers by purchasing 1000 copies of every published book for distribution to every free library in the country.

On average, Norwegians spend 500 kroner annually on purchasing books. Literary giants from Norway include Henrik Ibsen and Knut Hamsun. Snorri Sturluson's Heimskringla, or The History of Kings, dates back to the period between 750 and 1300 ACE and is a bestseller in Norway even today.

Grandiosa Frozen Pizza

The unofficial national dish of Norway is the Grandiosa Frozen Pizza. It is the highest-sold brand in the country. As per the latest statistics, the nation's 5.3 million citizens (the population of Norway is only a fraction of that of the US) eat nearly 47 million Grandiosa pizzas every year.

The US has a role to play in the story of the Norwegian Grandiosa. In the early 20th century, Italian immigrants to the US opened pizza shops all over the country. One such illiterate Italian immigrant was Frank Pepe. He and his wife opened Pepe's Pizzeria in 1925, and Louis Jordan, an employee, honed his pizza-making skills there.

He moved to Norway with his wife Anne, whose ancestors were Norwegians. In May 1970, Louis Jordan and his wife opened their first pizzeria in Oslo, Peppes. Pizzas were perfect for pepping up the unassuming food scene in Norway at that time. Following the success of Peppes, Grandiosa opened its shop in the 1980s and soon overtook Peppes as the country's largest-selling and most popular pizza brand.

Aquavit - Norway's Favorite Drink

Aquavit is a potato-based spirit that is seasoned with various combinations of cumin seeds, orange peel, dill, caraway seeds, and star anise. The name Aquavit traces its origins to 1931 when a bottle of Eske Bille's whiskey labeled "aquae vitae," or the "water of life," was sent to Archbishop Olav Engelbrektsson. The contents of this bottle promised to be a "cure for all ills."

The use of spices and herbs depends on the local cuisine and preferences. In Norway, Aquavit is meant to be sipped slowly like wine so you can experience the barrel-aged quality and the flavors of the herbs and spices.

Vinmonopolet - the Norwegian Way to Responsible Alcohol Drinking

Vinmonopolet has been the state monopoly for alcohol distribution since 1939. It is the only approved body to sell alcohol in Norway through approved distributors and suppliers appointed and licensed by the body. About 300 Vinmonopolet-licensed liquor stores in Norway are involved in the retail distribution of spirits, wine, and strong beer (any beverage with a 4.5% alcohol volume).

The purpose of the state monopoly through Vinmonopolet outlets is two-pronged. One is to limit the sales of alcohol to minimize profit, and the second purpose is to spread the importance of responsible drinking. There are no advertisements or discount offers available. Aquavit is also sold only through Vinmonopolet.

Skol Is "Cheers" in Norway

Before downing Aquavit, it is essential to shout "Skol" or "Skal." Even more important is to maintain eye contact with your co-drinkers during the shouting of "Skal." Maintaining eye contact is believed to have come from the days of the Vikings, who believed it to be extremely useful to keep an eye on others so that you are always prepared to deal with potential threats, even during celebrations.

Freia - the Famous Chocolate Factory in Norway

This famous chocolate brand was founded in the year 1889 by Olaf Larsen and Fredrik

Wilhelm Hjorth Christensen in 1889. With this factory, the two confectioners created Norway's confectionery history. Freia was Roald Dahl's inspiration for his book, "Charlie and the Chocolate Factory."

The Nobel Prize for Peace is Norway's to Give

Alfred Nobel, the inventor, and global industrialist born in Sweden, wrote in his will that the Nobel Prizes for medicine, physiology, chemistry, and physics were to be awarded from Stockholm, Sweden. But the Nobel Prize for Peace should be awarded from Oslo. All aspects of the peace prize are handled by the Norwegian Nobel Committee, which the Norwegian Parliament appoints.

There is no clear explanation as to why Alfred Nobel wanted this arrangement. Some people speculate that this could be because Norway and Sweden were in a union during his time. The union was dissolved in 1905, four years after the first prizes were given away.

Salmon Sushi Is Norway's Gift to Japan

Sushi is definitely Japanese in origin. But they did not use salmon in sushi until Norway introduced this option. In the 1980s, some Norwegian delegates to Japan suggested using salmon, and since then, it has been one of the most commonly used fish in Japanese sushi. Salmon sushi is particularly popular among the younger Japanese population.

Japan was unable to meet its high demand for fish, thanks to overfishing there. So, with Norway's suggestion, and its capacity to export seafood in plenty to Japan, salmon in sushi became a great choice. The salmon deal created in the 1980s is one of the reasons for the exponential growth of Norway's seafood exports which is today one of the country's largest industries.

Everyone in Norway Knows the Income and Wealth of Everyone Else

Information about the wealth and income of all Norwegians is available in the public domain. Three important figures, including annual income, tax paid, and total wealth, are culled out from the annual tax returns filed by all Norwegians. These figures are then published in the public domain for anyone to see.

Until 2013, this information was completely transparent and searchable. However, after 2013, a person can find out who has accessed their wealth-related information. That is the only change and the information is still available in the public domain! That's transparency at its peak!

The logic for this transparency is easy to understand. It is primarily to curb tax evasion. If you declare a low income to pay low taxes but living an openly rich life with a huge house and fancy cars, taxmen and other authorities will have doubts and can easily access your wealth-related information. Further, it makes it easy for the media to announce the list of the richest Norwegians annually.

Norway Is a Winter Olympics Star

Unsurprisingly, Norway is the most successful country in the Winter Olympics. It has won more medals (368 medals after the 2018 Olympics in South Korea) than any other country in the world in Winter Olympics history. The country hosted the sporting event twice, in 1952 in Oslo and in 1994 in Lillehammer. The Lillehammer Olympics resulted in the country's Olympic Museum, which still attracts tourists today.

It is a common joke in the country that all Norwegians are born with skis. However, the reason for the country's phenomenal success is more than that. Over 10,000 local clubs encourage Norwegians to learn, practice and participate in winter sports events, including skiing. Nearly 93% of Norwegian children participate in winter sports. And the best thing is that young children are encouraged to take part not so much to compete but for the fun of the sport. Slowly but surely, when the fun becomes an integral part of their psyche, passion comes in, and the desire to excel kicks in. With this attitude, medals come easy.

The Christmas Tree at Trafalgar Square Comes from Norway

Every year, for Christmas, a carefully chosen 50-60-year-old Norwegian spruce is sent to London to light up Trafalgar Square as a gesture of thanks to England for their help during WWII. The Christmas tree is taken from the forests surrounding Oslo. The felling of this tree, which happens in November, is also a celebratory ceremony that takes place in the presence of the Mayor of Oslo, the Lord Mayor of Westminster, and the British Ambassador to Norway. When the tree arrives in Trafalgar Square, it is lit with white lights and placed prominently so no one misses it.

Hydroelectric Power Powers Norway's Homes

While oil and natural gas are used in industries and other places, Norway's residences and homes predominantly (98% of the homes) use hydroelectric power.

Norway Offers Delectable Cuisine

Although nothing specific comes to mind when you think of Norwegian cuisine (except Aquavit), there is little doubt that the food and drink you get in this country are delectable and unforgettable. Thanks to its long coastline, the seafood is mouthwateringly fresh. The world's highest sushi restaurant is in Svalbard. Norwegians are skewed towards savory rather than sweet.

The local favorites include rye bread, various smoked meats, smoked and pickled fish (pickled herring is a common breakfast item for Norwegians), and cheese. A popular Norwegian cheese is a brunost, a brown whey cheese.

The Oldest European Musical Tradition

The Sami "yoik" or "joik" is a form of ululation believed to be the oldest musical tradition in all of Europe. The composer of "joik" is called a "joiker," and each composition is very personal to the composer. The Samis believe that the gift or skill of "joik" was given to them by the fairy folk of the Arctic regions.

Ten Interesting Facts about Norwegian Culture

1. Norway has a 100% literacy rate.
2. Norway allowed women to vote in local elections from 1907 and in national elections from 1913.
3. The universities and government-run state colleges offer free education to international students.
4. The cheese slicer was invented in Norway by Thor Bjorkland way back in 1925.

5. Norwegian passports have a picture of the Aurora Borealis embedded in them, which is revealed only under UV light.

6. Norwegians take a break for four weeks every summer, during which time they rest and/or go on fishing trips.

7. Ireland and Norway have been connected since ancient times. The Norwegians founded Ireland's capital Dublin in 836 ACE.

8. Norway turned off national FM radio stations in 2017. However, local stations continue to entertain listeners.

9. Norway was the first country to give paternity leave to fathers.

10. Roald Dahl, the famous writer of children's stories like "Charlie and the Chocolate Factory," "Matilda," and more, was born to Norwegian parents, although his birthplace was Wales.

Chapter Two - Norwegian History

The first human migration to Norway is believed to have happened after 7000 BCE. The Ice Age is believed to have ended around this time resulting in the regions around present-day Norway and other Scandinavian areas becoming habitable. The earliest Norwegians survived by hunting deer, seals, and elks and by fishing.

Farming came to Norway around 3000 BCE when they used stone tools and weapons for their farming and other daily needs. Bronze began to be used around 1500 BCE. The first forms of writing, the famous runes, are believed to have come into existence around 150 ACE.

Bronze Age in Norway

In the Bronze Age (between 1700 to 500 BCE), the region around present-day Norway witnessed rapid development, as with the other cultures of the world. The strong bronze tools and weapons (more powerful than stone) helped the Nordic people to build better and more permanent settlements and constructions. They built small dwellings and large longhouses.

They transformed from nomadic and semi-nomadic to permanent settlers with homesteads and farms. Again, thanks to improved farming tools made with bronze, agriculture became more sophisticated than before and became a common profession among the Nordic people, along with fishing.

Iron Age in Norway

After bronze, tools made of iron brought even better development and improvement to the Nordic people. Many more forest areas were cleared for agriculture, and the population grew thanks to increased yields and harvests. A new social structure developed in Scandinavia. Families joined together to form clans, and clans protected their members from other clans.

Conflicts were resolved by elderly freemen who assembled at predesignated sacred places to pass judgments and sentences. This process was called "thing," and this word continues to be used to refer to council chambers.

Norway and the Roman Empire

After 1 ACE, the Roman Empire began to exert a lot of influence in Scandinavia. Norwegians created the rune alphabet, and their trades with the Roman Empire included luxury items such as furs and skins. Powerful farmers became tribal chieftains whose power increased as Germanic people from other parts of Europe began migrating to Norway and its surrounding areas between 400 and 550 ACE. Local farmers sought protection from powerful chieftains from invading immigrants.

The Vikings of Norway

During the 9th century, Norwegian Vikings, like their Danish counterparts, were sailors and navigators and were also notorious for their raids on English, French, Irish, and Scottish villages and territories. The Norwegian Vikings also invaded Muslim-occupied Spain.

However, the Vikings from Norway not only invaded and raided European territories, but some of them also settled in these places. The Norwegian Vikings settled in different parts of

Scotland, including the Hebrides, Shetland, and the Orkney Islands. They also settled in other areas of England and Ireland, including the Isle of Man.

Bjarni Herjólfsson, a 10th-century Norwegian sailor, is believed to have been the first European to have sighted the shores of North America way back in 986 ACE when his ship was blown off course as he was sailing from Iceland to Greenland. How Present-Day Norway Came Into Being

During the early part of the 9th century, Norway broke away into its various factions and kingdoms. Bringing them together under one ruler came to be the job of Harold Fairhair, who got control over the entire west coast of this country and was called the "King of Norway" for the first time. Eric Bloodaxe and Haakon I was the succeeding Kings of Norway after Harold Fairhair.

Yet, the first "effective" King of Norway is credited to King Olaf Haroldsen towards the end of the 10th century. Where Haakon I failed in his attempt to convert the country to Christianity, King Olaf Haroldsen succeeded in doing so. From 995 to 1000, he converted the entire western coast of Norway to Christianity, and by 1030, all the inland areas also became Christian. He was canonized in 1035, and the king-turned-saint, St. Olaf, became the patron saint of Norway. Some of the top Norwegian rulers are:

Harald Fairhair - Also known as Harald the Fairheaded, he was the leader of one of two Viking forces battling against each other in the Battle of Hafrsfjord in 872 ACE. He was a harsh and cruel ruler despite being strong enough to unify Norway. Many Norwegians migrated to other countries, including Great Britain, Greenland, and Iceland during his reign.

The Middle Ages in Norway

The 10th and 11th centuries were largely peaceful in Norway, thanks to the riches that the Vikings came back with. But the rules of succession were quite ambiguous, which led to civil war in the country in 1130, with the church taking sides in different battles. Finally, in 1217, Håkon Håkonsson set up clear and unambiguous rules of succession.

The population increased significantly through the 11th and 12th centuries, and farms began to be divided into smaller parts. Many small landowners handed over their land to bigger landlords or the king during challenging times. The Golden Age of Norway is believed to have been around the 13th and 14th centuries, when peace reigned and international trade with Germany and Britain improved the economy and the lives of Norwegians. Then, the Black Death that hit Norway in 1349 brought an abrupt end to the peace and prosperity of the nation. A third of Norway's population died within a year. Multiple communities were entirely wiped out. Lower taxes made the king weak, and the church became exceedingly powerful.

Denmark-Norway Union

The Kalmar Union between Denmark, Sweden, and Norway was formed in 1397. While Denmark was able to pull out of the union soon enough, Norway was too weak to do so. Norway remained weak until 1520, when Denmark and Norway formed an alliance wherein the twin nations were ruled from Denmark's Copenhagen.

This continued until the 17th century when Denmark was caught up in multiple territorial wars leaving Norway in peace to develop a strong economy contributed by its timber trade, although Norway was still a Danish province. After the Battle of Leipzig in 1813, Christian Frederik, the resident viceroy of Norway, began a movement towards an independent Norway resulting in the Norwegian Constitution being written and adopted on May 17, 1814, the day Norway celebrates as Constitution Day.

Churches of Norway

One of Norway's most important contributions to world architecture is the invention of wooden churches. These unique structures look straight out of a fairy tale. Only 28 exist today out of the many thousands built during the medieval ages. The wooden churches of Norway are often compared and found to be similar to "terem" (separate living quarters built for the women of the Russian nobility of the Tsardom and the Grand Duchy of Moscow). Norway's wooden churches, which are also compared to witchcraft palaces and medieval castles, are a must-visit.

Some of the other beautiful churches and cathedrals in Norway that will blow your mind are:

- **The Arctic Cathedral** - Its stunning angelic structure resembling the Sydney Opera House attracts many tourists even though it was built as late as the 1960s.
- **The Nidaros Cathedral** - It is the oldest church in Norway, with its first structure built in the 11th century. It is located in the center of Trondheim city.
- **Borgund Stave Church** - This architectural marvel was built between the 12th and 13th centuries, and despite its small size, its unique profile makes it a popular tourist destination.

The Oldest Postal Services

The Norwegian Postal Service was established in 1647. The first post office was established on 17 January 1647 by Hannibal Sehested - Danish governor of Norway at that time, which was the start of the Royal Norwegian Post Office. Henrik Morian was given the contract and responsibility to run the post office for an annual fee. In 1719, the state took control of post offices.

In 1827, the Norwegian Post Office acquired two steamships to improve postal services along the coast and overseas as well. When train services started in Norway in 1854, postal services got a big boost as the train services supported postal services immensely. The first Norwegian postal stamp was issued in 1855.

Impeachment of the Norway Government

In 1884, nearly all the people in positions of power were convicted. The number convicted was so high that the king had to step down too. From then on, Norway has been a parliamentary democracy. Also, in 1898, voting rights were given to all Norwegians except those receiving poor relief. Norway was under Swedish control until 1905. When the Swedes withdrew, the head of state was voted by the people. With this vote, Prince Carl of Denmark was elected head of state as King Haakon VII.

Roald Amundsen - the First Person to the South Pole

Freia chocolates played a big role in Roald Amundsen's trip to the South Pole, the first ever by a human being. Freia chocolates provided for his sustenance throughout his trip. He started his education by studying medicine. But soon, he shifted his entire focus to polar research. He also flew over the North Pole in a plane first and the second time on an airship.

Skiing Is a Norwegian Invention

The modern form of skiing originated in Telemark in the 19th century. However, ancient rock carvings found in the regions in and around present-day Norway prove that skiing existed even 4000 years ago. The oldest excavated ski is proven to be 2300 years old. Sondre Norheim is credited with being the father of modern skiing. In the late 19th century, he used stiff ski bindings to help him jump and swing with a lower risk of falling. He then designed the Telemark ski, the precursor to modern skis.

Immigration of Norwegians to America and Improved Economy

In 1835, Norwegians began migrating to North America in search of a better life. By 1930, nearly 800,000 Norwegians had moved to North America, particularly settling in the American midwest. During the late 19th century, the economy of Norway improved significantly, thanks to improved infrastructure facilities and agricultural technologies, including in the realm of dairy farming.

Norway and World War I and World War II

Norway chose to remain neutral during WWI. Yet, the Germans sank nearly half of the Norwegian fleet killing over 2000 sailors. In WWII, it also, Norway chose to remain neutral, which did not prevent Germany from attacking the country and taking control of it in April 1940. Norway was under German control right through WWII. And moreover, being neutral did not keep Norway and its people safe in any way. Kirkenes, a mining borough, was completely destroyed by war strikes. The destruction of Kirkenes was the worst in all of Europe.

**Famous Modern and Contemporary
Norwegians**

Some of the famous post-medieval and
contemporary Norwegians who have made a
name for themselves and the country are:

- **Evard Grieg** - a musician and
  composer par excellence, Evard Grieg
  was inspired by Norwegian folk music.
  He created masterpiece music for
  Ibsen's masterpieces "Peer Gynt" and
  "In the Hall of the Mountain King."
  His debut concert was a record of sorts
  as it was the first in the old to have only
  Norwegian composers and musicians.
- **Edvard Munch** - the famous painter
  whose works include "The Scream"
  and others in the Frieze Series of the
  1890s, was born in Ådalsbruk, Norway.
  He is considered to be a remarkable
  figure of Norwegian Expressionism
  and Symbolism.
- **Øystein Wiik** - a popular Norwegian
  actor, novelist, singer, and songwriter,
  Øystein Wiik was born in Oslo. He
  played lead roles in multiple musicals,
  including Les Misérables' as Jean

Valjean in Vienna, London, Oslo, and Munich.

- **Henrik Ibsen** - Born in Skien Municipality, Norway, Henrik Ibsen, the famous playwright, is considered to be the "Father of Realism." His famous works include "A Doll's House," "Ghosts," "Peer Gynt," and more.
- **Knut Hamsun** - Hamsun's literary works span 70 years. His books include "The Hunger," "Mysteries," "Pan," and more. He won the Nobel Literature Prize in 1920

Ten Interesting Facts about Norwegian History

1. King Olaf V was a sportsman. He won a gold medal in the 1928 Olympic Games in sailing. He was an active sailor right throughout his life. He was known for his down-to-earth attitude and even often took public transport to inspire the Norwegians to reduce pollution by using public transport.
2. Norway is not an official member of the European Union, although it was a founding member of the UN. The first

secretary-general of the UN was a Norwegian. Trygve Lie held this powerful and respected position from 1946 to 1952.

3. The first emigration from Norway to the US happened in July 1825 when 52 crew and passengers boarded the Restauration from Bergen Harbor and landed on the shores of Lake Ontario in October 1825.

4. The prototype of the now ubiquitous aerosol spray can be invented by Erik Rotheim, a Norwegian, in October 1926.

5. Despite everything, Henrik Ibsen never won the Nobel Prize for Literature.

6. Roald Amundsen died doing what he loved the most, exploring. He died on a rescue mission in 1928

7. Knut Hamsun is considered to be the "leader of the Neo-Romantic Revolt" that started around the turn of the 20th century.

8. The Holmenkollen Ski Festival is the oldest in the world. It has been in existence since 1872 and continues to attract one million visitors annually even today.

9. Today, the number of post offices in Norway is 30, and 1400 outlets exist in retail stores.

10. Edvard Munch also painted the staff dining room at the Freia Chocolate Factory.

Chapter Three - Norwegian Geography

On the east, Norway shares land borders with three nations, namely Russia, Finland, and Sweden. The Barents Sea flows in the north of Norway. On the west, the coasts of Norway are washed by the North Sea and the Norwegian Sea. The Skagerrak Strait in the south separates Norway and Denmark.

Norway is a constitutional monarchy consisting of the Prime Minister and the Statsråd, the Council of State. Kingship is hereditary. The legislature of Norway is called Storting or Stortinget.

The flag of Norway is a blue (with white outlines) cross on a red background. The colors represent the earlier unions of Norway with Sweden and Denmark. The red and white represents their union with Denmark, and the blue stands for its union with Sweden.

The Languages of Norway

Norway has two official languages, namely Norwegian and Sami. Norwegian has two dialects including, Bokmål and Nynorsk, both of which are very different from each other. Nynorsk or Landsmaal developed in the 19th century and is used mostly in the rural areas of the western fjord region. But most Norwegians use Bokmål rather than Nynorsk.

In schools, children are taught both versions of the Norwegian language. The national broadcaster also publishes news in both versions. Official forms and documents are available in both versions too. Norsk is the Norwegian way of saying the name of the Norwegian language. Norge is Norway in the Norwegian language. The country is known by other names in different European languages, including:

- Norja (in Finnish)
- Norwegen (in German)
- Noruega (in Portuguese and Spanish)
- Norvegia (in Italian)
- Norvege (in French)

Elk - Norway's National Animal

Elk is one of the largest of the deer family. Along with reindeer, elks are the most commonly visible animals in Norway. Called "elg" in Norwegian, they are the biggest land animals found in the country. Their antlers can grow up to 1.5 m, while some can grow up to 2.3 m in height. The Samis domesticate elks, especially the ones you strolling on the roads in the north of the country. To see elks in the wild in Norway, you will have to visit one of the national parks in the country.

The World's Longest Road Tunnel

The world's longest road tunnel stretching for over 24 km, is in Norway. The Lærdal Tunnel in Vestland County of Norway connects the towns of Aurland and Lærdal. It takes 20 minutes on average to pass through this tunnel. On the topic of tunnels, Norway also holds the record for having the deepest undersea tunnel in the world. The Eiksund Tunnel is at a depth of 942 feet below sea level and runs for a distance of over 7700 m. Some fun facts about the Lærdal Tunnel:

- The lighting in the tunnel varies at regular intervals to offer varied views, break the monotony, and help reduce the strain on the drivers.

- A cave every 6 km separates the different sections of the road.
- An ample number of cameras at strategic locations counts the number of cars entering and exiting the road facilitating swift responses in case of accidents and breakdowns.
-

Kirkenes Lies More to the East Than Finland

Kirkenes, a small Arctic town in Norway, is just 15 km from the Russian border. Norway's land border with Russia is nearly 200 km long, although there is only one road crossing. The Storskog crossing is Europe's northernmost road border crossing. In 2017, a tunnel and a bridge were opened on the Norwegian side of the crossing to decrease travel time.

The crossing is quite busy as people from both sides travel to either side to buy stuff. The Norwegians go to the Russian side to buy cheaper fuel, and the Russians come to the Norwegian side to buy good quality food and other items in Kirkenes.

Interestingly, Kirkenes is as far to the east as Cairo. Its closeness to the Russian border means there is a lot of Russian influence in this beautiful town that is also a popular tourist attraction. Bilingual street signs are common all over Kirkenes. English is a commonly spoken third language here, considering there are more international visitors than locals. The local shops have advertisements, offers, and deals targeting visiting Russians.

Grimstad - the Sunniest Place in Norway

Grimstad is the home of Henrik Ibsen, the writer of many famous works, including A Doll's House, Ghosts, and Peer Gynt.

Northern Norway Never Sees the Sun in Winter

The country's moniker, the Land of the Midnight Sun, is derived from the polar nights Northern Norway experiences right through winter. In the same way, during summer, this part of the country does not experience sunsets. On the topic of sunlight and Norway, Rjukan and Viganella do not have sunlight for six months every year. These two regions are nestled deep inside valleys so that the mountains around them prevent sunlight from entering their areas. The locals have found a way around this. They use giant mirrors placed strategically in the mountain ridges to enjoy the warmth of reflected sunlight.

Norway's Coastline Is Long and Beautiful

Norway's coastline extends over 25,000 km and is home to several fjords, inlets, and beaches spanning three seas: the Barents Sea, the North Sea, and the Norwegian Sea. It stretches from Oslofjord in the south, weaves in and out through numerous fjords on the western side of the country, moves northward, and finally bends around the Scandinavian peninsula to seamlessly become part of the Russian coastline.

The Hurtigruten coastal voyage is the best way to see and enjoy the spectacular Norwegian coastline. This 12-day voyage starts from Bergen to Kirkenes and then takes you back to Bergen. Norway is the largest exporter of salmon in the world and also the largest seafood producer in the world.

The Stunning Fjords of Norway

One of the country's most visited spots is its stunning fjords on the west coast. Some of the best and most renowned ones are:

- **Sognefjorden** - Sognefjorden extends 205 km from the ocean and has a maximum depth of 1308 m, the deepest fjord in the world. On the inland side, it extends into the Jostedalsbreen and Jotunheimen National Parks. The average width of Sognefjorden is about 4.5 km.
- **Nærøyfjord** - This fjord is an arm of Sognefjorden. It is named after Njord, the Norse sea god. Some parts of this fjord are so narrow that you can actually reach out and touch the waterfalls from the deck of your cruise ship. A 2-hour cruise between Flam and Gudvangen is the perfect way to enjoy the sights of Nærøyfjord.
- **Geirangerfjord** - Geirangerfjord's majestic mountains, peaceful waters, stunning waterfalls (Bridal Veil and Seven Sisters), and beautiful flora will definitely take your breath away. This

15-km fjord is a UNESCO Heritage Site.

Bouvet Island - the World's Most Remote Island

Although uninhabited, Bouvet Island, the most remote island in the world, is under Norway's administrative jurisdiction. This island houses an automated meteorological station that researches penguins, their population, and their way of life, including their hunting strategies. Lars Christensen's 1927 exploration team landed on Bouvet and claimed it for Norway.

It is an obscure inactive volcano that is completely covered in ice and is located thousands of miles away from any mainland in the South Atlantic Ocean. The only humans visiting Bouvet Island are the research scientists undertaking occasional expeditions. However, life does exist here in the form of multiple species of Antarctic seabirds and penguins who have made this remote island their home.

The Samis of Norway

Around 1% of the total Norwegian population comprises the Samis. Who are the Samis? They are an ancient indigenous group living in the Scandinavian areas of Finland, Sweden, Norway, and Russia's Murmansk region. Half of the world's Sami population lives in Norway.

Until the 20th century, the Samis lived their tribal, semi-nomadic way of life according to their belief systems, hunting, fishing, and grazing deer. Even today, many of the Samis are engaged in reindeer-related industries. The belief systems of the Samis are rooted in Shamanism and nature worship. They worshiped spirits, including ancestor spirits and sacred stones, which they called "sejds."

The Sami Shamans are called "Nojds" and are believed to know how to reach and navigate the spiritual world. Like other forms of Shamanism, the Sami shamans also believe in helper spirits, celebrate shamanic festivals, and engage in other shamanic practices. They also teach others who want to learn about Shamanism.

Hardangervidda Plateau

This Norwegian plateau holds the record as a shelter for the largest herd of wild reindeer in all of Europe. Europe's largest herd of wild reindeer lives in Hardangervidda Plateau. The Hardangervidda Plateau is Europe's biggest plateau. The National Park here includes high mountains, lush valleys, vast plateaus, waterfalls, and amazing fjords.

The wild reindeer population in winter can go up to 25,000 in the entire country, and about 7000 of these animals can be found in this plateau.

Norwegian Mountains

Nearly 2/3rd of Norway's landscape consists of mountains. Round rock formations and craggy summits are an unmissable part of the country's landscape. More than 300 mountain peaks are over 2000m above sea level here. Most of the mountains in Norway have flat tops, which indicate that they once upon a time used to be plains at sea level. This idea or hypothesis came from one of the most famous Norwegian geologists, Hans Henrik Reusch, and of course, several studies conducted by other geologists. Here are some of the stunning mountains in Norway:

- **Galdhøpiggen** - The highest peak in Norway, Galdhøpiggen stands at 2469 m tall and is located in the Jotunheimen National Park in the Jotunheimen Mountains.
- **Glittertind** - The second highest peak, standing at 2465 m tall, is also located in Jotunheimen Mountains and is a close neighbor of Galdhøpiggen.
- **Store Skagastølstind** - This is the third-highest peak in Norway, standing at 2405 m, and is located in the Hurrungane range.
- **Snøhetta** - Another tall peak in Norway is Snøhettawhich has a height of 2286 m. It is located in the Dovrefjell mountain range.
-

Other important mountain peaks in Norway include Kjerag, Skarstind, Gaustatoppen, and many more. An interesting aspect of mountaineering in Norway is that nearly half of the Norwegian population has access to a private cabin (they refer to these cabins as "hytta"). For the others, staffed mountain lodges called Fjellstuer are easily accessible. That's how much the Norwegians love their mountain peaks.

Oslo Is Norway's Capital City

Oslo is also the most diverse city in the country, with immigrants from different parts of the world calling it home. The largest number of immigrants in Oslo are of Pakistani origin. Others are from Poland, Sweden, and Somalia. The Norwegian TV drama called Skam had a lot to say about the diversity of Oslo. The show has many fans worldwide, thanks to numerous translations available on YouTube (not all of these translated versions are official, though).

Despite being an urban area, a large portion of Oslo consists of untouched forests called Oslomarka, which are easily and quickly accessible by public transport. Oslomarka is protected, and no development is allowed here. These forests are home to several species of beaver, wolf, lynx, and moose. Many locals head for summer hiking trails and winter skiing spots on weekends.

For a while, Oslo was called Christiania after King Christian IV ordered the city to be rebuilt after it was destroyed by fire in 1624. Oslo was restored as the city's name in 1925. Oslo's name is Tiger City or Tigerstaden.

While the city center and many residential areas are on the mainland, Oslo consists of many islands that can be reached by hourly passenger ferries. These islands have plenty of tourist destinations.

Norway's Rail Journeys

While the road trips in Norway are unbeatable, the rail journeys are no less. You will be treated to sublime scenery as your train charmingly chugs along. The Flam Railway, or "Flamsbana," is one of the most popular routes. It starts from Myrdal Station in the mountains and descends down to the charming village of Flam, traveling 20 km and passing through 20 tunnels. It descends a distance of 865 m through twisty and steep curves in the Flam Valley.

The sights that beckon you include snow-capped mountains, small farms clinging to the edges of the hills, rippling rivers, and stunning waterfalls. The train goes slowly, allowing travelers and tourists to capture the beauty their eyes see onto their cameras for posterity.

Norway's Flora and Fauna

Talking about Norway's wildlife has to begin with polar bears, which outnumber humans in Svalbard, a remote archipelago. Other animals that inhabit Norway include walrus, the Arctic fox, reindeer, Eurasian lynx, and a horde of sea life. Birds that can be found in Norway include the clown-faced puffin, penguins, etc.

The largest part of Norwegian forests is filled with boreal coniferous trees, primarily the Norway spruce and Scots pine. Common plants that you will find in Norway include the common coleus, red elderberry, Rugosa rose, common ash, etc.

Ten Interesting Facts about Norwegian Geography

1. Norway has only one active volcano, Beerenberg. This volcano standing at 2227 m above sea level, is the northernmost volcano in the world. Located midway between Norway and

Greenland, there are no inhabitants there, although science expeditions and cruise ships stop there for a while.

2. In Svalbard, Norway, bears outnumber people.

3. Minnesota is the unofficial capital of Norway in the United States. More Norwegians live here than in any other part of the US.

4. The Norway-Svalbard islands have more than 1100 fjords. The longest river in Norway is Glomma

5. Troll is a research station in Antarctica that continuously monitors toxins in the environment, radiation, meteorology, and seismology. It was built by Norway in 1990. It continues its operations today and is also the base starting point for glaciological and geological fieldwork.

6. There is a town in Denmark named Hell. With over a thousand residents, this interestingly named town is close to the Trondheim International Airport. It even has its own train station.

7. The largest glacier in the world, Jostedalsbreen (with an area of 487 square km), is in Norway.

8. Erling Kagge, a Norwegian, is the first person to travel alone and unaided to the South Pole. He did this feat in 1993.

9. Sami Shamanism is officially recognized in Norway.

10. The Trolltunga Peak has the shape of a troll's tongue and earned the epithet of being "one of the most instagrammable" destinations in the country.

Chapter Four - Popular Norwegian Tourist Attraction Trivia

Norway is home to gorgeous, jaw-dropping natural beauty and dramatic, stunning landscapes that will take your breath away at every turn. From the magical Northern Lights to the remote but beautiful Svalbard to excellent cruises that take you through the vistas of the western coast to great hiking trails, there's something in Norway for all kinds of travelers.

Norway is a dream destination for many travelers across the globe. And yet, there are so many places to see that deciding which to see and which to leave out can be a challenge, especially for those who cannot make more than one trip to this magical nation. Still, here are some of the top and popular tourist destinations to help you arrive at a decision aligned with your time and resources.

Hurtigruten Coastal Voyage

This 12-day, 1255-km round trip runs from Bergen in the south to Kirkenes in the north and back. It is one of the best ways to soak in the stunning sights offered on the western coast of Norway.

The best thing about this voyage is that you do not need to be tied down entirely. You can hop on and hop off for certain sections of the cruise. You can also stop off to discover the various ports on the way. It is a perfect cruise to explore the western coast of Norway. Here are some facts that will help you decide your preference for taking this unmissable voyage while in Norway:

- Summer is the most popular time for these voyages, although you are likely to have to deal with huge crowds, and the prices will be at a premium. The cost of the voyage is at its peak between June and August. During winter, the prices get more economical, and you will also get some good deals and offers.
- Climate change along the coastline happens drastically and almost always without warning. Find out the weather

conditions before you book your tickets. And regardless of the season or time of the year, you can definitely expect some precipitation and winds at some or the other points in your voyage.

- During summer, all voyages sail into Geirangerfjord; in the autumn, Hjørundfjord is included in the itinerary.

Vinnufossen Falls

The Vinnufossen Falls is the highest waterfall in Europe, falling from a height of 860 m. It is also the 6th highest waterfall in the world. The water in this cascade falls in four stages before reaching the bottom of the valley. It is best viewed during the summer months between June and August.

Starting at Vinnubreen glacier, this waterfall is just 6 km from Sunndalsøra and is a perfect place to get some stunning photos. While you can see the waterfall from a distance, you can also get close to it by following a marked and well-cleared path from a picnic spot in the area called Holsskeiet. A 20-minute walk on this path will take you close to Vinnufossen Falls. Other beautiful waterfalls in Norway include Vøringsfossen in the Hardangerfjord Region, Vettisfossen Waterfalls, the Seven Sisters Waterfall, and more.

Jotunheimen National Park

This national park is aptly called the "Home of the Giants." Two of the highest mountain peaks in Norway, namely Galdhøpiggen and Glittertind, are found here. Jotunheimen National Park is recognized as Norway's premier fishing and hiking region, covering over 1100 square km. It was established in 1980 by a royal decree.

The wildlife that you will see in Jotunheimen National Park includes elk, wolverines, reindeer, and lynx. The lakes and rivers in this park have a lot of trout too. Over 200 mountain peaks are found in this region. Researchers found a 1500-year-old Viking arrowhead in the south of Norway, driven by climate change in the Jotunheimen National Park area.

Guided tours are available for those seeking to hit the hiking trails to reach these mountain peaks.

National Scenic Routes

18 routes are designated National Scenic Routes in Norway because they offer some of the most stunning views of nature as you drive through them. These routes, also called National Tourist Routes, contribute to the fact that road trips in Norway are unbeatable. Government funding is used to improve the road conditions and facilities these routes offer. Your trip to Norway is incomplete if you don't travel at least on a few of these routes promising spectacular views. Here are some important pointers before you begin:

- Some of the roads are closed during winter because of poor weather and high altitudes.
- The time you take to travel cannot be decided only by the driving speed and distance. Happy uncertainties like stopping to capture splendid vistas, sightseeing, pit stops, and more need to be included.

Some of the best and most popular National Scenic Routes of Norway are:

Geiranger-Trollstigen Route

With eleven hairpin bends, the sights on this road are one of the most popular in Norway. Norwegian nature offers the best views at the Geiranger end of this route. Multiple viewing platforms at strategic locations give you the perfect and secure vantage points to enjoy this National Tourist Route's stunning views. The road is carved into the mountain wherever possible, and in places where you need to climb up, stone roads have been built. This road opens at the end of May and closes by October or November, depending on the intensity of the onset of winter.

Hardanger Route

This 158-km route gives you splendorous views of orchards that line the Hardangerfjord. The pleasure of the journey is enhanced by the sights of impressive waterfalls and the fresh fruit that you can buy directly from the local farmers. This National Tourist Route has four sections: Granvin - Steinsdalsfossen,

Norheimsund - Tørvikbygd, Jondal-Utne, and Kinsarvik-Låtefoss.

To travel between Kvanndal-Utne and Utne-Kinsarvik and between Jondal and Tørvikbygd, you have to use the car ferry to cross over the fjord. This scenic route is open throughout the year. However, the section through the Hardangervidda mountain plateau may be closed during winter if the weather is bad. The perfect time to drive through the Hardanger Route is during spring, the height of flower and fruit blossoms.

Hardangervidda Route

This drive is across the largest mountain plateau of northern Europe. The advantages of this already excellent road include crossing the splendidly scenic and steep Måbødalen valley and Eidfjord, the fjord side village. This 67-km National Tourist Route connects the Hardangervidda Mountain Plateau (at the height of 1250 m) to the shores of the Hardangerfjord. Part of this route passes through the Hardangervidda National Park.

Ryfylke Route and Jæren Route

This 260-km journey envelopes diverse landscapes from high mountains to dense forests to deep fjords. The Ryfylke Route is also one of the most diverse, covering the best of Norway's fjords, multiple stunning islets and islands, lush farmlands, sheer cliffs, and more. The southern end of the Ryfylke route is home to Norway's famous tourist landmarks like the Kjerag boulder and Preikestolen or the Pulpit Rock.

Jæren is Norway's agricultural heartland and is the main attraction on the Jæren National Scenic Route. The Jæren landscape is filled with miles of sandy beaches, sand dunes, stark scenery with boulders, and salmon-filled rivers. Intensive agriculture in this region makes it Norway's food basket.

Norway's Hell

As mentioned in one of the earlier chapters, Hell is a little Norwegian town. The train station with the bold-lettered sign declaring the village's name is a popular photo destination. When you visit this place, you will find the station buzzing with tourists clicking photos, and you will do it too. Hell is warm and welcoming, replete with local souvenir shops, shopping centers, and hotels, among other facilities.

Incidentally, the word "Hell" comes from the Norse word "hellir," which means "cliff cave" or "overhanging." The English "hell" is connected with the Norse underworld "Hel," ruled by Hel, the underworld goddess.

However, Hell is more than just the name. Within walking distance from the train station, you will find a place with rock carvings of reindeer. These carvings discovered in 1895 are believed to be more than 5000 years old, dating back to the Stone Age! It is also the place where the annual Blues in Hell festival is held.

And despite the name, the village of Hell in Norway is very peaceful, replete with typical Scandinavian houses made of wood, well-trimmed gardens, and plenty of cyclists.

Svalbard

Though a little far-flung, Svalbard, one of the northernmost inhabited places in the world, is a great place to visit, especially if seeing polar bears in the wild is your thing. Svalbard's nickname is the "Realm of the Polar Bears." Nearly two-thirds of this Arctic haven is protected under the umbrella of reserves, national parks, and sanctuaries. Despite its remoteness, here are some compelling reasons for you to visit Svalbard:

- Svalbard means "cold shores."
- Svalbard is an archipelago of remote Arctic islands, the main ones being Spitsbergen, Nordaustlandet, Edgeøya, and Barentsøya. Many other smaller, outlying islands are also part of Svalbard.
- Spitsbergen is the largest island of Svalbard. Interestingly, Svalbard was known as Spitsbergen earlier.
- Thanks to the Gulf Stream, Svalbard is not entirely locked in by ice, and the waters around the west and south of this remote archipelago are relatively ice-free.

- The best way to see Svalbard is from an expedition vessel.
- In summer, the sun doesn't set in Svalbard. You can always see the sun from April 19th through to August 23rd, and this is the reason for Norway's moniker, "Land of the Midnight Sun."
- During winter, one night lasts for three months. The opposite of the midnight sun is the polar night when you will not see a sunrise for three months.
- Svalbard is the best place to see the Northern Lights (more on this later)
- With a little over 3000 people living in Svalbard, there are inhabitants from over 50 countries here, which means it is easily the most diverse place in the world in terms of percentage.
-

Svalbard Is Home to the World's Four Northernmost Settlements

The four settlements include Longyearbyen, Ny-Ålesund, Pyramiden, and Barentsburg, all of which are in Spitsbergen, Svalbard's largest island. Longyearbyen (the first place you will land in when you visit Svalbard) is the primary settlement, with a little over 2000 people calling it home. Like any other urban town, it has all facilities, including shops, hotels, and even an international airport.

Barentsburg is the second largest settlement in Svalbard, with a population of 470, mostly Ukrainians and Russians. Ny-Ålesund is a settlement consisting of only research scientists. It lies further north of Spitsbergen. During summer, the number of people in this settlement increases to 120. Otherwise, not more than 35 people call Ny-Ålesund home. Pyramiden is the fourth settlement, and only a handful of people live here to run hotels and act as tourist guides.

Norwegian Olympic Museum

The Norwegian Olympic Museum is an ultra-modern one filled with exciting stuff to do, experience, and watch. Here, visitors can experience unforgettable, goose-bump-inducing Olympic moments of world-class Olympians from all over the globe. The history of the Winter Olympics is a delight to behold.

This museum is located in Lillehammer, the 1994 Winter Olympics Games host. The two Norwegian Olympic Games held in Oslo and

Lillehammer are hugely contributory in the Norwegian Olympic Museum. You get to see original objects used in the games, including medals. There is a biathlon simulator you can try your hand at.

Norway's Northern Lights

The Northern Lights are a spectacle not to be missed if you are traveling to Norway, especially during winter. Other than the stunning beauty of these colorful lights, here are some fascinating facts about Aurora borealis that take place about 100 km above the earth:

Today, we know the science behind the appearance of the Northern Lights. But, in ancient times, human beings were bewildered and frightened. They used legends and myths to understand nature. According to Norse legend, the Northern Lights are the reflections of the shields and armors of the Valkyries, the formidable warriors of Norse mythology.

Scientifically speaking, the Northern Lights are seen because of distortions in the earth's magnetic field. The particles and gases in the atmosphere get charged and are released as photon energy. Although they can appear at any time, they are visible only in the dark. This is why you must get away as far as possible from cityscapes for optimal sightings. The place for the best view of the Northern Lights changes. When you visit the country, research, find out the best place to get the highest chances of sighting these wondrous lights, and then make your travel plans.

The Briksdal Glacier

The Briksdal Glacier is an arm of the biggest glacier in Europe, the Jostedal Glacier. Starting at the height of 1200m, the Briksdal Glacier comes down spectacularly through the narrow Briksdalen Valley and flows into the lake at the bottom. It is one of the most popular tourist attractions in Norway. You can indulge in multiple activities while at the Briksdal Glacier and the surrounding national park.

You can hit the hiking trail. The 2.5km trail is flat with a few small inclines and relatively easy to do. The first part of the hike is the most difficult. Once that is over, the hike becomes easy, and the pleasure you get from the stunning vistas will take your breath away.

You can take the troll cars. The farmers from Oldedalen would transport people to the Briksdal Glacier by horse carriages. But, in 2004, troll cars were installed. These open-air vehicles airlift people and drop them near the glacial lake. However, from the place of drop, there is a 10-minute walk to the glacier.

Trollstigen - Driving through Stunning Mountain Vistas

Trollstigen is one of the most beautiful mountain passes you can drive through. Full of hairpin bends, Trollstigen is a perfect tourist activity, though it is unavailable in winter. The scenery is so beautiful that the road trip itself is a popular tourist destination. Mighty mountains surround Trollstigen. There are Mount Bispen, Mount Kongen, and Mount Dronninga in the west and Mount Stigbottshornet, and Mount Storgrovfjellet in the east.

The starting point of this mountain pass is the same as the Geiranger-Trollstigen national scenic route. On the way, you will see the spectacular views of the Gudbrandsjuvet gorge amidst other mountainous landscapes. You can also take a ferry trip across the Nord Dalsfjord.

Ten Interesting Facts about Norwegian Tourist Attraction

1. Pyramiden, the fourth and smallest settlement in Svalbard, is a former Russian mining town that was abandoned when the Soviet Union was disbanded.
2. Longyearbyen is just over 800 miles from the North Pole.
3. The Global Seed Vault (Doomsday Vault) opened in 2008 and is in Svalbard. It holds copies of all the seeds in the world. It is to ensure against loss of food grains in case of a global crisis.
4. The Northern Lights also play a part in Chinese legends, although sightings are very rare in China due to their latitudinal position. On rare occasions when these lights were sighted, the Chinese created their own legends and believed that these lights represented the battle between good and evil dragons.
5. In some parts of Europe, such as Italy, France, and the British Isles, the Northern Lights were believed to be a

bad omen indicating an outbreak of a disease or war.

6. The first photograph of the Aurora Borealis was taken on 05 January 1952 by a German astronomer and physicist, Otto Rudolf Martin Brendel.

7. Atlanterhavsparken Foundation in Tuenset, Troldhaugen, Norway, houses an aquarium that has the largest collection of saltwater fish in the world. The views of this spectacular aquarium open into the vast ocean.

8. Tromsø, a city in Northern Norway, is often the most popular place to visit to see the Northern Lights in all their splendor.

9. Ten of the 30 highest waterfalls in the world are in Norway.

10. You can board a ferry or take a kayak to get a close-up view of the Seven Sisters waterfall.

Norwegian Quiz

Now that you have read so much trivia about Norway, it is time to test yourself on how much you know about this magically wonderful country steeped in natural beauty and rich history. So, here goes:

Questions

1. What is the name of the highest mountain peak in Norway?
2. What is the background color of the Norwegian flag?
3. What is the capital of Norway?
4. Which is the largest center in Svalbard?
5. From which country did Norway gain independence in 1905?
6. What is the name of the Norwegian king who won a gold medal in the Winter Olympics?
7. Which two Norwegian cities hosted the Winter Olympics?
8. What is the population of Svalbard, approximately?
9. With how many countries does Norway share a land border?
10. Which is the longest river in Norway?
11. What do Norwegians call their country?
12. Which day is celebrated as Constitution Day in Norway?
13. Who was the first king to rule over a unified Norway?

14. Which fish did the Norwegians introduce for Japanese sushi?
15. Which is the largest glacier in Norway?
16. What is the name of the famous Norwegian alcoholic drink?
17. Which Nobel award is given in Oslo?
18. What is the currency of Norway?
19. Which famous Norwegian painter painted "The Scream?"
20. What is the official name of Norway?
21.

Answers

1. Galdhøpiggen
2. Red
3. Oslo
4. Longyearbyen
5. Sweden
6. King Olav V for yachting in the 1928 Olympics
7. Oslo and Lillehammer
8. Less than 3000
9. Three; Sweden, Finland, and Russia
10. River Glomma
11. Norge
12. May 17th
13. King Harald Fairhair
14. Salmon

15. Jostedalsbreen
16. Aquavit
17. Nobel Peace Prize
18. Norwegian kroner
19. Edvard Munch
20. Kongeriket Norge, or Kingdom of Norway

Conclusion

Norway is not just beautifully stunning but also one of the happiest places on earth. According to the World Happiness Report published by the Happiness Research Institute of Denmark, Norway is one of the happiest countries in the world. The annual reports from the Global Peace Index also state that Norway is a peaceful and safe country.

With peace, safety, happiness, and stunning natural beauty to boot, what can prevent any person who loves to travel from visiting Norway? Use the information in this book to learn as much as you can about this wonderful country. Learn a few important and useful words in Norwegian and go and explore the fjords and mountains of this gorgeous country.

Here's one last interesting Norwegian tidbit before concluding this book:
Svalbard has only 25 miles of road!

One last word from the author

Of all the books to choose from, thank you very much for choosing this trivia book and reading all the way to the end!

If you think the book has lived up to your expectations (or more), you are welcome to write that in a review. Likewise, if you thought the book contained only things you could have easily found on Google or YouTube, I'd love to know!

What to read next: If you enjoyed this book, check out the other books in the Scandinavia Trivia Series!

References

"10 Fascinating Things You Didn't Know about Aquavit." Liquor.com, www.liquor.com/articles/10-facts-about-aquavit/.

"11 Fun Facts about Oslo, Norway." Life in Norway, 16 Feb. 2019, www.lifeinnorway.net/oslo-facts/.

"120 Norway Facts: The Land of the Midnight Sun." Turn Your Curiosity into Discovery - Facts.net, 24 Feb. 2020, facts.net/norway-facts/.

Albert, Daniel. "Roald Amundsen: 11 Fascinating Facts about the Norwegian Polar Explorer." Life in Norway, 24 July 2022, www.lifeinnorway.net/roald-amundsen-facts/.

Allsop, Chris. "Norwegian Culture: 9 Fascinating Customs & Traditions | Celebrity Cruises." Celebrity Current, 8 Jan. 2021, www.celebritycruises.com/blog/norwegian-culture.

"Driving Norway's 18 National Scenic Routes." Life in Norway, 20 Oct. 2017, www.lifeinnorway.net/national-tourist-routes/.

"Flåm Railway : Norway Travel Guide : Nordic Visitor." Norway.nordicvisitor.com, norway.nordicvisitor.com/travel-guide/attractions/the-fjords/flam-railway/.

"Geiranger-Trollstigen National Tourist Route." Www.visitnordic.com, www.visitnordic.com/en/attraction/geiranger-trollstigen#.

Gordon, Ilana. "How a Frozen Pizza Brand Became Norway's Unofficial National Dish." Atlas Obscura, 17 Apr. 2018, www.atlasobscura.com/articles/frozen-pizza-national-dish-norway.

Gupta, Gaurav. These 10 Churches in Norway Beckon You. 6 Dec. 2021, traveltriangle.com/blog/churches-in-norway/.

"Hardanger National Tourist Route." Www.visitnordic.com, www.visitnordic.com/en/attraction/hardanger-national-tourist-route.

Navitskaya, Alisa. "10 Fun Facts about Norway." Medium, 6 Jan. 2022, blog.triptile.com/10-fun-facts-about-norway-157cfee9b927.

Nikel, David. "17 Fascinating Facts about the Northern Lights." Life in Norway, 1 Nov. 2020, www.lifeinnorway.net/northern-lights-facts/.

---. "21 Fascinating Facts about Norway." Life in Norway, 15 Feb. 2019, www.lifeinnorway.net/norway-facts/.

---. "A Brief History of Norway." Life in Norway, 20 Feb. 2019, www.lifeinnorway.net/history-of-norway/.

---. "Bouvet Island: The World's Most Remote Island." Life in Norway, 24 Nov. 2022, www.lifeinnorway.net/bouvet-island/.

---. "Trollstigen: Driving Norway's Famous Mountain Pass." Life in Norway, 16 Aug. 2020, www.lifeinnorway.net/trollstigen-norway/.

"Norwegian Scenic Route Jæren." Www.visitnorway.com, www.visitnorway.com/places-to-go/fjord-norway/the-stavanger-region/listings-stavanger/norwegian-scenic-route-j%C3%A6ren/7207/#.

"Norwegian Scenic Route Ryfylke." Www.visitnorway.com, www.visitnorway.com/listings/norwegian-scenic-route-ryfylke/238452/.

"Not Just Snow: What's the Secret to Norway's Winter Olympic Success?" The Guardian, 17 Feb. 2022, www.theguardian.com/sport/2022/feb/17/secret-behind-norway-winter-olympic-success.

"Our History." Postennorge.no/En, www.postennorge.no/en/about-us/history#.

private, Environmental certification of, et al. "Norwegian Olympic Museum." Www.visitnorway.com, www.visitnorway.com/listings/norwegian-olympic-museum/5453/.

secretatlas. "50 Interesting Svalbard Facts to Inspire Your Visit." Secret Atlas, 8 Mar. 2022, www.secretatlastravel.com/explorers-club/svalbard/svalbard-50-interesting-svalbard-facts-to-inspire-your-visit/.

Src="https://Secure.gravatar.com/Avatar/2d8a8e4eaf135692a17ea52b3163b250?s=57, img Alt=, et al. 10 Informative Facts about Jotunheimen National Park | Isolated Traveller. 17 Apr. 2020, www.isolatedtraveller.com/10-informative-facts-about-jotunheimen-national-park/.

team, Norway Excursions. "Exploring the Incredible Briksdal Glacier." Norway Excursions, 13 Mar. 2020, www.norwayexcursions.com/en/blog/exploring-the-incredible-briksdal-glacier/#.

"Vinmonopolet, Tender Process, Systembolaget, Tender Requests." Concealed Wines, www.concealedwines.com/business-opportunities-scandinavia-wine-producers/vinmonopolet-the-norwegian-monopoly/.

"Vinnu Waterfall." Www.visitnorway.com, www.visitnorway.com/places-to-go/fjord-norway/northwest/listings-northwest/vinnu-waterfall/11835/.

"Welcome to Hell (in Norway)." Life in Norway, 5 July 2014, www.lifeinnorway.net/hell-norway/.

"Wildlife & Animals in Norway | Norway Travel Guide." Norway Travel Guide, 13 Feb. 2015, norwaytravelguide.no/norwegian-nature/animals-and-wildlife-in-norway

Please consult a licensed professional before attempting any techniques outlined in this book.

By reading this document, the reader agrees that under no circumstances is the author responsible for any losses, direct or indirect, that are incurred as a result of the use of information contained within this document, including, but not limited to, errors, omissions, or inaccuracies.